P9-DOA-665

Malala Yousafzai

Peachtree

ROBIN S. DOAK

Children's Press®
An Imprint of Scholastic Inc.
New York   Toronto   London   Auckland   Sydney
Mexico City   New Delhi   Hong Kong
Danbury, Connecticut

Content Consultant
James Marten, PhD
Professor and Chair, History Department
Marquette University
Milwaukee, Wisconsin

Library of Congress Cataloging-in-Publication Data

Doak, Robin S. (Robin Santos), 1963-
 Malala Yousafzai / by Robin S. Doak.
   pages cm. -- (A true book)
 Includes bibliographical references and index.
  ISBN 978-0-531-21191-5 (library binding : alk. paper) -- ISBN 978-0-531-21205-9 (pbk. : alk.
paper) 1. Yousafzai, Malala, 1997---Juvenile literature. 2. Girls--Education--Pakistan--Juvenile
literature. 3. Girls--Violence against--Pakistan--Juvenile literature. 4. Women social reformers-
-Pakistan--Biography--Juvenile literature. 5. Taliban--Juvenile literature. 6. Pakistan--Social condi-
tions--Juvenile literature. I. Title.

 LC2330.D63 2015
 371.822095491--dc23   2014030978

No part of this publication may be reproduced in whole or in part, or stored in a retrieval system,
or transmitted in any form or by any means, electronic, mechanical, photocopying, recording, or
otherwise, without written permission of the publisher. For information regarding permission,
write to Scholastic Inc., Attention: Permissions Department, 557 Broadway, New York, NY 10012.

© 2015 Scholastic Inc.
All rights reserved. Published in 2015 by Children's Press, an imprint of Scholastic Inc. Published
simultaneously in Canada. Printed in China 62.
SCHOLASTIC, CHILDREN'S PRESS, A TRUE BOOK™ and associated logos are trademarks and/or
registered trademarks of Scholastic Inc.
1 2 3 4 5 6 7 8 9 10 R 24 23 22 21 20 19 18 17 16 15

**Front cover: Malala in Birmingham,
United Kingdom**

**Back cover: Malala holding her Anna
Politkovskaya award in 2013**

Find the Truth!

Everything you are about to read is true *except* for one of the sentences on this page.

Which one is **TRUE**?

T or F Malala is the youngest person ever to win the Nobel Peace Prize.

T or F Malala has returned to Pakistan in order to fight for education.

Find the answers in this book.

3

Contents

THE **BIG** TRUTH!

Malala's Family

Malala's father has said
that she was meant to
"fly high in the sky."

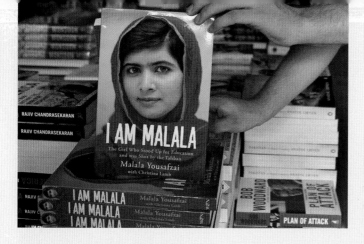

Malala's autobiography is an international bestseller.

3 Dark Days

How did Malala recover from the attempt on her life?

4 The Fight Continues

What is Malala doing to spread her message today?

Malala is a role model for young women all around the world.

Malala Yousafzai has
become an inspiration to
girls around the world.

CHAPTER 1

Growing Up in Pakistan

In 2012, a Pakistani teenager named Malala Yousafzai was shot and nearly killed by a member of a **terrorist** group. The crime made headlines around the world. People everywhere were shocked and angered. How did Malala become a target for **assassination**? All she had done was stand up for her belief that girls in Pakistan should have access to education.

 Only three out of every five girls in Pakistan between the ages 15 and 24 are able to read and write.

Early Years

Malala Yousafzai was born on July 12, 1997, in Mingora, Pakistan. Mingora is the only city in the Swat Valley, a region in the northwestern part of the country. It is just 90 miles (145 kilometers) away from the border of Afghanistan. Like other Pakistanis, the people who live in the Swat Valley are **Muslims**. They follow the traditions and beliefs of **Islam**.

The busy streets of Malala's home town, Mingora

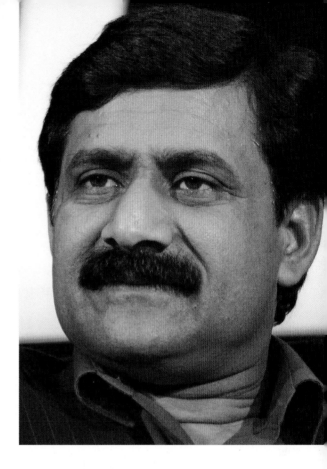

Malala has a very close relationship with her father.

Proud Parents

Malala was the first child of Tor Pekai and Ziauddin Yousafzai. When she was born, people expected her parents to be disappointed. In Malala's part of the world, boys are considered more important than girls. But Malala's family felt differently. Her father was especially proud of his new daughter and her big, intelligent eyes. Ziauddin took his daughter everywhere he went. She sat on his lap and listened to his stories and conversations.

Ziauddin sometimes received death threats for his views on education.

Some people in Pakistan believe that only boys should be allowed to attend school.

Emphasis on Education

Literacy and education are important in Malala's family. To promote education in the Swat Valley, Ziauddin founded a school. He believed that knowledge is the most important thing in life. With education, people can overcome poverty and hatred. He believed that education should be available for all Pakistani children—girls and boys alike. Ziauddin became known in the Swat Valley as someone who spoke out for education and civil rights. People warned him to be quiet, but he never stopped.

Mother and Daughter

Malala had a special bond with her father, but she also looked up to her mother. Tor Pekai followed the Islamic custom of **purdah**, which calls for women to be kept out of the sight of men. When she went outside, Malala's mother wore covering from head to toe and a veil to hide her face. Although she had never been educated herself, Tor Pekai encouraged Malala's interest in learning. She also taught her daughter to speak up for herself and be independent.

Women who follow purdah cover as much of their bodies as possible when leaving the house.

A Love of Learning

As she grew up, school became Malala's favorite place. She loved attending classes and learning new things. She was smart and very competitive. She also loved sports, art, and drama. But Malala worried that soon she would be expected to stay inside so men could not see her, like her mother. She knew that this was not the way she wanted to live.

Malala was named for a legendary hero named Malalai.

Malala was smart and curious as a young girl.

Pakistan

Pakistan became a nation in 1947 after it separated from India. It was founded as a place where India's Islamic people could settle together. The new nation saw a great deal of violence and bloodshed in its early years. Relations between Pakistan and India were tense. The two countries went to war in 1947, 1965, 1971, and 1999. In recent years, Pakistan has been faulted for testing nuclear weapons and allowing terrorists to live there safely.

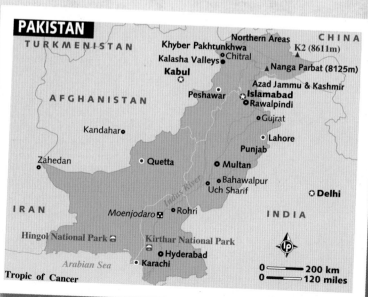

13

The Taliban uses violence to make people follow its rules.

CHAPTER 2

Fighting for Change

When Malala was a teenager, her homeland became a battleground. A group called the Taliban began using violence to take over the Swat Valley. As they gained more power, life changed for the valley's people, especially women and girls. People who dared to stand up to the Taliban were often murdered. The group also began blowing up schools that taught girls. Many people were afraid, and they remained silent.

The Taliban enforces a strict set of religious rules known as Sharia law.

15

Extreme Views

The original Taliban is an **extremist** Muslim group that was founded in the nearby country of Afghanistan. It ruled Afghanistan with an iron fist, forcing men and women to follow strict codes of behavior. The Taliban also supported al-Qaeda, another violent Islamist organization. Al-Qaeda was responsible for the September 11, 2001, terrorist attacks against the United States.

Before the United States invaded Afghanistan, the Taliban was not very active in Pakistan.

Women had little choice other than to follow the rules of purdah after the Taliban took control of the Swat Valley.

The Taliban Takes Over

After the September 11 attacks, the United States invaded Afghanistan. Hundreds of Taliban members took shelter in Pakistan. Some people welcomed them and embraced their strict rules. Later they formed a Pakistani Taliban. As the years went on, the Pakistani Taliban grew in power, and in 2007 they seized control of the Swat Valley. They told people to destroy their televisions. Women were warned to stay at home. People who disobeyed the Taliban's many rules were whipped in public. Sometimes they were even killed.

Boys were able to continue attending school under Taliban rule.

Malala dreamed of someday becoming a doctor. She knew that if she left school, this dream would die.

Breaking the Rules

With the Taliban making the rules, life changed for 10-year-old Malala. The group ordered all girls to drop out of school and stay at home. Most girls obeyed. They were afraid of the Taliban. But Malala and her friends did not follow the rules. They kept going to school every day. They hid their books beneath their shawls and wore their school uniforms beneath loose clothing.

Spreading the Message

Malala began to speak out against the new rules. In September 2008, Ziauddin arranged for her to give a public speech in front of reporters. In the speech, she asked, "How dare the Taliban take away my basic right to education?" Later, she appeared on a Pakistani television show to spread her message. Many people thought Malala was brave, but some were worried. By speaking up, Malala had attracted the attention of the Taliban.

This school was destroyed by the Taliban because it taught girls.

19

Going Online

In early January 2009, the Taliban announced that all girls' schools would be closed down. Malala was determined to do something about it. On January 3, she began writing a diary about her experiences living under Taliban rule. She and her father sent the diary to the British Broadcasting Corporation (BBC). The BBC published it online as a blog.

Malala's blog detailed the stress of living under the Taliban.

To protect Malala, her name was changed to Gul Makai, or "Corn Flower," in the blog.

A group of Pakistani girls look through the window of their closed-down school.

Not Quite Average

In the blog, Malala wrote about her fears for her safety and her dreams for the future. Readers got to know an extraordinary young woman. In many ways, Malala was just like other teens around the world. She loved reading the Twilight books and worried about her hair. But she was also the voice of thousands of young girls who weren't allowed to go to school.

Malala's blog turned her into a worldwide celebrity.

Malala in the Spotlight

Malala's blog soon had readers all around the world. In 2009, a journalist from the *New York Times* came to her school to film a movie about her. The film showed Malala's last days at Ziauddin's school before it was closed down. It was a huge success, and it attracted even more attention to Malala's cause.

Changing the Rules

People in Pakistan and around the world added their voices to Malala's. They demanded that girls be allowed to attend school. In response, the Taliban lifted the education ban—but only for girls ages 10 and younger. Older girls were still expected to stay at home. Malala had an easy solution for this. She pretended she was 10 instead of 11.

Many people followed Malala's lead in demanding equal education rights.

WE WANT EDUCATION In SWAT

Malala's Family

Malala's family is a big part of her life. Her parents taught her the importance of standing up for her beliefs, while her younger brothers have supported her through her most difficult struggles. Thanks to their help, she has been able to spread her message about the need for equal education rights all around the world.

Ziauddin
Ziauddin is Malala's number one supporter. As a poet and a teacher, he believes strongly in the value of education. Today, he often travels around the world to collect awards for his daughter. He also speaks on her behalf when she cannot attend certain events.

Tor Pekai

Tor Pekai, Malala's mother, is very proud of her daughter's accomplishments. Although she is unable to read and write herself, she has always supported Malala's desire for education. Tor Pekai is very religious. Only recently has she allowed herself to be photographed with Malala.

Khushal

Khushal is two years younger than Malala. Like many siblings, the two often argue and bicker. In her autobiography, Malala writes, "Never in history have Malala and Khushal been friends." But she admits that she missed her brother when they were apart.

Atal

Atal is seven years younger than Malala. Malala describes him as active and bright-eyed, "like a squirrel."

The Pakistani military fought to drive the Taliban out of the Swat Valley.

CHAPTER 3

Dark Days

In July 2009, the Pakistani army announced that the Taliban had been driven out of the Swat Valley. In August, Malala and her friends returned to school. But the Taliban had not been defeated. Many people in Pakistan still supported them. In the coming months and years, they continued to use violence against those who challenged them. But no one could have guessed at the violence they were planning for Malala.

In August 2009, a U.S. attack killed the head of the Pakistani Taliban.

27

Teen Activist

Malala was back at school, but the fight wasn't over. She kept speaking out for what was right. She took part in student gatherings. She also learned how to collect facts and write news stories. In December 2011, she was awarded Pakistan's first National Peace Prize for standing up to the Taliban's unfair rules.

Malala was excited to return to school.

Malala did not want to give up the fight for education rights until all girls were allowed to attend school.

Refusing to Back Down

Malala's mother was not happy with the attention her daughter's work was attracting. Tor Pekai worried that the Taliban would try to silence her. Eventually, the Taliban began sending death threats to Malala. After that, even Ziauddin asked her to stop speaking against them. But Malala refused. She had a mission, and she would not be silent.

In Mingora, school buses are often made from converted trucks.

A Day Like Any Other

On October 9, 2012, Malala and her friends were riding the bus home from school. Malala noticed that the roads were strangely empty. Suddenly, the bus was stopped by three men standing in the road. One of them climbed aboard and asked the driver, "Who is Malala?" The driver refused to answer and told the man to get off the bus. Another man climbed in and asked the frightened girls the same question: "Who is Malala?"

A Horrible Tragedy

None of the girls answered, but several of them glanced toward Malala. She was the only student who didn't have a scarf covering her face. The young man raised a pistol, pointed it at Malala, and fired three times. The first bullet hit Malala on the left side of her face, just above her eyebrow. It traveled through her body and stuck in her shoulder. The other bullets wounded two girls sitting next to Malala.

This 3-D model shows how the bullet damaged Malala's skull.

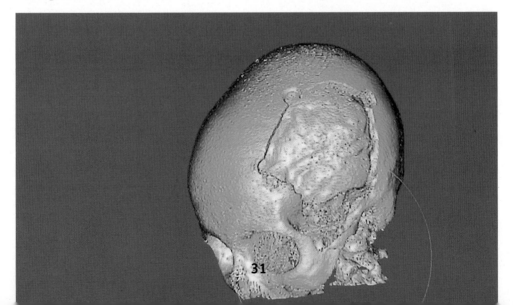

The Race to Save Malala

Malala was seriously wounded. The bus driver sped to the nearest hospital to get help. However, this hospital lacked the equipment needed to save her. After two hours, Malala was flown by helicopter to a hospital in Peshawar, the capital of Khyber Pakhtunkhwa province. There, doctors found that the bullet had passed very close to Malala's brain. She was lucky to be alive.

Because of her fame and accomplishments, Malala received the best medical care available.

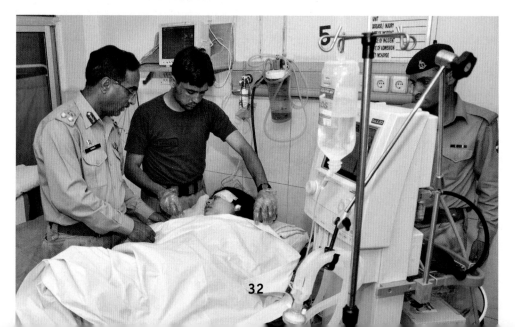

The plane carrying Malala touches down in Birmingham, England.

The leader of the United Arab Emirates donated one of his private planes for Malala's eight-hour flight to England.

Emergency Flight

In the evening, Malala's condition worsened. It seemed that the brave young girl might not survive. Doctors performed surgery to help her live. But even after this surgery, they weren't sure how much damage the bullet had done. Would Malala ever be able to speak or walk again? Would she be the same brave girl she had been before? The doctors decided to send Malala to a special hospital in England.

Treatment in England

The hospital in England was heavily guarded to prevent terrorists from trying to harm Malala. Already, the Taliban had promised to try again if Malala survived. They had even threatened her brothers.

Malala finally woke up a week after the shooting. She was in a strange new country, and she had no memory of the attack. She did not know what had happened to her.

Timeline

October 9, 2012

Malala is shot as she rides the bus home from school.

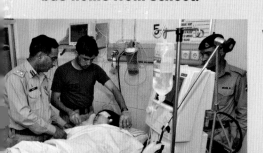

October 15, 2012

Malala is flown to a hospital in Birmingham, England.

Worldwide Support

As Malala recovered in the hospital, well-wishes poured in from every part of the world. She received cards, flowers, chocolates, and stuffed animals. People followed news of her progress as she relearned how to walk and talk. She had operations to fix her damaged left ear and the **paralyzed** left side of her face. Malala was now focused on one thing: getting better so she could go home.

October 16, 2012

Malala wakes up for the first time since the shooting.

January 2013

Malala is released from the hospital.

People around the world held gatherings to show their support for Malala.

MALALA YOU ARE THE PRIDE

36

CHAPTER 4

The Fight Continues

The Taliban tried to silence Malala and frighten other people who spoke out against them. But the attack ended up having the opposite effect. It made Malala even stronger and more fearless. As her story made international headlines, it inspired others to speak out for education and women's rights. People around the world lifted up their hands and said, "We are Malala."

Pakistan's peace prize was named the Malala Prize in honor of its first winner.

A New Home

In January 2013, Malala was released from the hospital. She and her family missed Pakistan, but it was too dangerous to return. Instead, the family settled in an apartment in England. Malala and her brothers started attending school there. Ziauddin took a job as the United Nations special advisor on global education. Still, the family misses their friends and home back in Pakistan.

Malala gives a speech outside a library in Birmingham.

Once a week, Malala Skypes with her friends to keep up with events back home.

President Barack Obama and his family met with Malala in 2013.

International Hero

Today, Malala is one of the most famous activists in the world. Her picture has appeared on the covers of countless magazines and newspapers. She has appeared on TV shows that are broadcast all over the globe. She has also had the chance to talk with many important leaders. She has met then president of Pakistan Asif Ali Zardari, Queen Elizabeth II of Great Britain, and U.S. president Barack Obama.

Spreading the Message

Malala even found time to write a book about her experiences. The book, which was released a year after the shooting, is called *I Am Malala*. The title is the answer to the question her attackers asked the people on the bus. At the beginning of the book, she dedicates her story to "all the girls who have faced injustice and been silenced." Together, she promises, they will be heard.

Malala's book has been sold around the world.

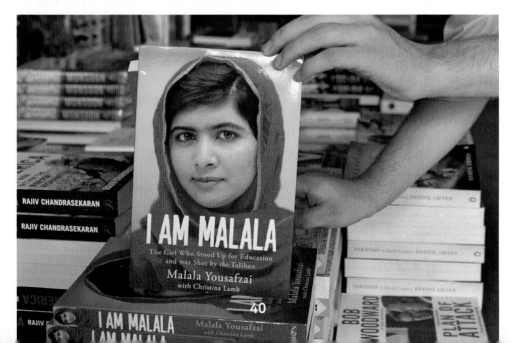

Malala's Big Speech

When Malala was in the hospital, more than half a million people signed an online petition to nominate her for the Nobel Peace Prize. This important award is given to one person or group each year. It honors the fight for world peace and justice. Malala was the youngest person ever nominated for the prize. She didn't win, but she was invited to make a speech before the United Nations Youth Assembly. At the end of the speech, she received a standing ovation.

Helping Those in Need

In 2014, Malala spoke out after an extreme Muslim group kidnapped about 300 girls from a school in Nigeria. Her organization, The Malala Fund, raised money for groups that support education and women's rights in Nigeria.

Sadly, not everyone supports Malala. In Pakistan, some Muslims criticize her for her refusal to be silent. The Taliban has promised to target her again if she returns home. Her book has even been banned by thousands of schools in Pakistan.

Malala autographs a copy of her book for a supporter at a 2014 event in London, England.

In 2013, Malala won the International Children's Peace Prize.

Malala is using her newfound fame and influence to inspire others to take action and make a difference.

Big Plans

In late 2014, Malala won the Nobel Peace Prize with Indian activist Kailash Satyarthi. At age 17, Malala was the youngest person ever to win. She stated, "I want to tell other children, all around the world, that they should stand up for their rights. They should not wait for someone else. . . When no one speaks, your voice gets so [much] louder, that everyone has to listen to it." Malala continues to use her powerful voice to make the world a better place. ★

Malala's birth date: July 12, 1997

Malala's birthplace: Mingora, Pakistan

Names of Malala's parents: Ziauddin and Tor Pekai Yousafzai

Names of Malala's brothers: Khushal and Atal

Title of book written by Malala: *I Am Malala: How One Girl Stood Up for Education and Changed the World (Young Readers Edition)*

Some of Malala's honors and awards: Named one of *Time* magazine's 100 most influential people in the world; Clinton Global Citizen Award; *Glamour* Woman of the Year; International Children's Peace Prize; International Prize for Equality and Non-Discrimination; Sakharov Prize for Freedom of Thought; honorary Canadian and Italian citizenships

Did you find the truth?

Malala is the youngest person ever to win the Nobel Peace Prize.

Malala has returned to Pakistan in order to fight for education.

Resources

Books

Aretha, David. *Malala Yousafzai and the Girls of Pakistan*. Greensboro, NC: Morgan Reynolds Publishing, 2014.

Sonneborn, Liz. *Pakistan*. New York: Children's Press, 2013.

Yousafzai, Malala. *I Am Malala: How One Girl Stood Up for Education and Changed the World*. New York: Little, Brown Books for Young Readers, 2014.

Visit this Scholastic Web site for more information on Malala Yousafzai:
★ www.factsfornow.scholastic.com
Enter the keywords **Malala Yousafzai**

Important Words

assassination (uh-sas-uh-NAY-shuhn) — the murder of someone who is well-known or important

extremist (eks-TREE-mist) — someone who holds extreme political or religious views

Islam (iz-LAHM) — the religion based on the teachings of Muhammad

literacy (LIT-ur-uh-see) — the ability to read and write

Muslims (MUZ-limz) — people whose religion is Islam

paralyzed (PAR-uh-lyzed) — helpless or unable to function

purdah (PUR-dah) — a tradition in certain societies that requires women to remain out of the sight of men

terrorist (TER-ur-ist) — someone who uses violence or threats in order to, for example, frighten people, obtain power, or force a government to do something

Index

Page numbers in **bold** indicate illustrations.

About the Author

Over the past 25 years, Robin Doak has written dozens of nonfiction books for children of all ages. Of the many people she has written about, Malala is one of the most inspiring. Doak lives in Maine with her husband, two dogs, and a cat named Lumpy.

PHOTOGRAPHS ©: Alamy Images: 4, 20, 24, 28 (epa european pressphoto agency b.v.), 43 (Scott Houston); AP Images: 11 (B.K. Bangash), 35 right (Courtesy of Malala Yousefzai), 26 (Pedro Ugarte, Pool), 19 (Sherin Zada); Corbis Images/Rashid Iqbal/epa: 14; Getty Images: 10, 17, 18, 29, 5 top, 30, 40 (Aamir Qureshi/AFP), 31 (AFP), 5 bottom, 25 top, 41 (Andrew Burton), 33, 34 right (Andrew Yates/AFP), 35 left, 36 (Arif Ali/AFP), 23 (Asif Hassan/AFP), 38 (Christopher Furlong), 8 (Hasham Ahmed/AFP), 3, 42, 44 (Karwai Tang), 13 (Lonely Planet), 6 (Mandel Ngan/AFP), cover (Paul Ellis/AFP), 12, 21, 22 (Veronique de Viguerie); Landov: 32, 34 left (ISPR/EPA), 9 (Reuters); Newscom/DDAA/Zob Wenn Photos: 25 bottom; Reuters/Luke MacGregor: back cover; The Image Works/Alex Macnaughton/Impact/HIP: 16; The White House/Pete Souza: 39.